THE EXCHANGE

GREED
for
SHORT SELLING

Edmund Jörg

THE EXCHANGE

GREED
for
SHORT SELLING

Bibliographic Information of the German National Library:
The German National Library lists this publication in the German
National Bibliography; detailed bibliographic data is available
on the internet at dnb.dnb.de.

New edition 2023
III.

© 2023 Edmund Jörg, Kempten/Allgäu formerly Frankfurt a.M.
www.edmundjoerg.de

Production and publisher: BoD - Books on Demand, Norderstedt

ISBN: 978-3-7528-9180-5

Table of contents

Foreword

The stock exchange is a fascinating world and a focal point for various financial interests. Laws, regulation/compliance and settlement modalities are the corset in which market participants have to operate, and they know the environment inside out.

The stock exchange is an integral part of our financial system; it is integrated into it and technically networked worldwide. With the increasing additional establishment of futures exchanges at the end of the last century and the automation of business processes as a whole that inevitably went hand in hand with this, automation of immense proportions resulted in succession, but these effects initially remained rather hidden from a broad public.

The introduction of index trading with the futures exchanges has not only revolutionised exchange trading technically. Along with this, the dynamics have also shifted more towards futures exchanges, and over-the-counter platforms have increasingly been able to establish themselves.

The price determination of all classic stock exchange orders is carried out continuously via electronic stock exchange platforms on high-performance EDP systems, and Deutsche Börse uses this to determine the DAX price index (German Share Index) every second. In order to be able to do this, the Exchange Rules prescribe the market maker model with compulsory quotation at all times. This inevitably results in short sales, in the sequence of which the short seller has delivery obligations.

It must be seen with concern that a general use of short selling at any time and probably also increasingly in connection with securities lending activities contributes to the fact that the securities market can work efficiently, but thus also becomes highly sensitive and more price-sensitive.

The shares proportionally backed in an index unit form a bought or sold share basket that can only be closed by closing out or by cash settlement at maturity. Interdependencies with the cash market are close, and the tradability of an index based on indices determined and published online by the exchange for cash and futures trading ensures that a certain consistency of price quotations prevails in the indices across all markets and time zones. This inevitability is thought provoking. Basically, it makes almost no difference from where price developments take their course, the change of a price component in an index-relevant share or in the index itself, like a communicating tube, ensures that a constant immediate equalisation takes place here.

Computer networking therefore not only ensures that trading is always possible, but also that price fixing is possible both in the share and in the index.

A price swing in an underlying share, however determined, is immediately included in the index calculation; on the other hand, every price change in the index causes immediate market price changes in all underlying shares themselves.

Additional market price risks beyond the regular stock exchange trading of supply and demand, which is solely and exclusivly supported by market making to determine the market price, arise from non-owners as short sellers as well as from market participants who are focussed on pure index trading; also to be mentioned in this interplay are the effects from derivatives trading, which constantly and increasingly determine price movements as well as thin out the cash market.

Short selling, index and derivatives trading are to be considered under this aspect; the market maker model for the ability to calculate an index at any time is the prerequisite for this.

This is elaborated and comprehensively explained, just as the connection of short sales to the always-necessary securities lending makes it clear, as the delivery of short sales would otherwise not be possible at all from a settlement point of view. The de facto undermining of the issued quantity of securities in circulation caused by short selling in the banking system, which is exactly determined when an issue is made, shows that ownership of a securitised security does not end even when securities are lent, as securities are still held in possession, but it leads to a book-entry closure of the volume of securities in circulation through the transfer of securities and to a concomitant reduction in the tradable securitised securities issue, which I will explain to you in detail. The explanations cannot and do not represent all information on short selling, securities lending and index trading and do not claim to be complete. The intention is to deal with the topic in a generally valid and brief but comprehensible manner for everyone, as well as to show how this sub-sector fits into the stock market environment and beyond.

In which fields is there a need for regulation? Knowing full well that hardly anyone wants to know anything about this, let alone that anyone is interested at all - not the people involved, not the financial industry, not the politicians and probably not even the financial supervisory authority BaFin itself.

The current market model is seen as inherent in the system, but it must be questioned because it is about the investor who is left behind. The issue is completely ignored here, as the need for regulation has supposedly been solved with the "crutch of covered short selling", good money is being earned and bubbling levies and taxes ensure peace and quiet.

Well, there is an immediate need for action. This topic drives me as an author. Other focal points are the functioning of the stock market in Germany with Deutsche Börse, the Eurex derivatives exchange and its settlement and clearing systems as well as the presentation of economic backgrounds.

"Elon Musk as CEO of SpaceX and Tesla, denounces short selling quite rightly". The clearly unlawful tradability of non-negotiable securities, not prohibited by BaFin and made possible worldwide by the EU Short Selling Regulation, causes the aforementioned unauthorised immobilisation of an issue.

Edmund Jörg, Kempten/Allgäu in April 2023

1.   Short selling

Basically, a securities short sale is the sale of securities that are not owned, also known as "shorting" or "going short".

Nowadays, this short selling is largely practised in the cash market, but it can also take place on the futures market.

The transaction is concluded as a spot exchange transaction or as a direct transaction with banks or by banks; furthermore, transactions are possible via the futures exchange as options or futures transactions with standardised terms and maturities extending far into the future.

As possible uses and main motives for short selling, I would like to mention first and foremost the speculation on price changes through more favourable repurchase opportunities, furthermore the price hedging of open securities positions as a hedging transaction as well as the arbitrage possibilities between the spot and the futures market.

Regarding short selling, however, the creation of liquidity through market making can only be mentioned for technical reasons; other activities are congruent with the main point mentioned at the beginning.

1.1 Delivery obligations

Like any regular sale of securities, it is also subject to the securities short sale to the same settlement procedure and a strict delivery obligation.

In Germany, for example, securities transactions concluded must be delivered two days after the transaction is concluded, according to stock exchange regulations.

The same applies internationally: in the Euromarket, delivery standards are also set at 2 days by the ICMA, the International Capital Market Association and the European Central Bank through Target2/T2S system for the central bank money side and the Central Securities Depositories for the remaining securities custody and services. It is run on the Eurosystem's Single Shared Platform (SSP).

In the event of a delay in securities delivery, a compulsory buy-in will take place, depending on the respective market. In the case of a German exchange transaction, this is 4 days after the value date, but until then the defaulting seller is charged penalty interest.

1.2 Risks of a short sale

When comparing a short sale with an actual shareholding, we must immediately realise that risks and opportunities are diametrically different, pronounced.

Whereas the risk of loss of actual share ownership is always limited to a maximum of the purchase price with an infinite possibility of profit, in the case of short selling the possibilities of profit are limited and the possibilities of loss are infinite.

After a sale, a short seller could be caught in a so-called short squeeze, which is characterised in particular by the fact that fewer securities are offered on the market than are demanded. The risk of this is to be assessed as "ultimately infinitely high" and cannot be hedged or even limited by the short seller by means of stop price guarantees or the like, because if no one is willing to return these securities to the market after short sales have taken place, this would ruin a short seller, because market prices can rise infinitely high.

1.3 Opportunity/advantage of a short sale

As already outlined under "Possible uses of and reasons for a short sale", it is primarily the attempted exploitation of more favourable redemption opportunities after a short sale has been made that is usually initiated by professional market players such as hedge funds, etc. And if the calculation works out, an often-considerable price gain can be collected. Equally, however, an investor could also be a short seller by selling short against an existing securities portfolio in part, in whole or in excess for hedging purposes in the event of price declines or expected poor economic figures. From a tax point of view, a private investor could use a short sale for hedging purposes without affecting the relevant "old holdings 2008" for withholding tax purposes. Furthermore, a variety of arbitrage opportunities between the cash market and the futures market can be exploited.

The technical sequence through market-making for price-setting purposes has already been mentioned before.

1.4 Short Selling Prohibitions in Germany

Short selling in Germany was once and again banned, in 1931 in the Great Depression, in 2010 in the financial crisis for financial stocks by BaFin, the Federal Financial Supervisory Authority[1], most recently for Wirecard shares in 2019. Today, however, it applies exclusively to the so-called "uncovered short sales", but not to non-owned securities in general, which can be settled by prior agreement based on a securities lending transaction. Conclusion: Short sales are possible in Germany under certain conditions.

1.5 Short Selling Ban on the FWB

It is in fact conditionally available for a small sub-segment; the conditions of the Frankfurt Stock Exchange (FWB) state this

---

[1] Short selling regulation from 27.7.2010, replaced by EU short selling regulation on 1.11.2012

in §104 Prohibition of Short Selling in Structured Products[2] , and it is exclusively related to these:

"Companies admitted to trading on the FWB may only sell structured products on the FWB if safe that at the time of the fulfilment of the transactions, they have, in accordance with the Conditions for Transactions on the FWB, the portfolio of securities required fulfilling the sale transaction. The portfolio according to sentence 1 must be ensured by purchase transactions already concluded at the time of sale or by the portfolio available at the company. In the case of financial commission transactions (Article 13 par. 1 no. 2) as well as in the case of trade brokering (Article 13 par. 1 no. 3), admitted companies shall ensure that clients for whom or for whose account they enter sell orders for structured products have at their disposal the portfolio of securities required for fulfilment pursuant to sentence 1".

This short sale order could serve as a blueprint for a Short-selling ban, but this would not even have to be enacted. The vehicle of the securities lending ban for short selling purposes would be sufficient to prevent short selling and thus make the EU Short Selling Regulation reducible to regulations on market making and liquidity provision.

---

2 FWB Exchange Rules as of 18.3.2013

1.6 Short selling bans internationally

During the financial crisis in 2010, for example, there were temporary short-selling bans only in financial stocks in France, Spain, Italy and Belgium; other eligible securities could still be sold short.

1.7 Relevant regulations

BaFin[3] -Allgemeinverfügung (General statement) as of 4.3.2010 plus supplements, in force since 27 July 2010 and replaced by: EU Short Selling Regulation of 29.6.2012, in force since 1.11.2012 and the WpHG[4] § 30, Notification and Publication Obligations with Exemptions for Market Makers, Liquidity Providers and Similar Persons.

1.8 Can anyone short sell?

Yes, but first let us take it one-step at a time. In general, the bank is obliged in any case to check for existing securities cover before selling securities, whereupon a binding sale of securities can be made.

---

3 Federal Financial Supervisory Authority, Berlin

4 Securities Trading Act

If a client has also concluded a necessary framework agreement in advance of a short sale, which, however, requires good creditworthiness and the ability to enter into forward transactions as well as sufficient deposited collateral (account balance/valued securities account balance), short sales can also take place and be released via securities lending agreements. However, it is understood that short sales entered into are subject to strict settlement regulations, including possible compulsory cover in the event of non-compliance. Additional attention must be paid to liquidity management, since domestic short sales are initially subject to a flat-rate tax of 30 % on the sales proceeds in the absence of available purchase price information.

2. Paradox of the short sale

Let us go back to a security itself, since it is only tradable on the stock exchange and thus capable of being delivered at all through the issue and the subsequent admission to trading.

The number of securities in circulation in the market is limited in principle in such a way that the number or nominal amounts are fixed, but they can never be changed by the market, not even by short selling.

The transferability of securities results from the securities certificate itself or from the content of the securities certificate. Nowadays, the transfer of ownership of securities usually takes place as a book-entry transfer at a securities clearing and deposit bank, so the delivery of actual physical securities can be left out of this consideration as a nostalgic memory.

The certificate held in collective safe custody, details of which are available in official, generally accessible securities publications (WM-Mitteilungen), provides precise information on the denomination, e.g. the smallest possible units or the nominal value.

If we now look at any share and know that this company XYZ, for example, has issued 10,000,000 shares, then this number of shares in circulation is centrally deposited at Clearstream Banking AG in Germany and held in collective safe custody there; dispositions are usually made by transferring securities from a collective portfolio. Strict compliance with the Custody Account Act across all custody levels ensures that third-party orders and overdrafts of custody accounts cannot occur, as these are not permitted.

The number of shares in circulation can also only be increased by a capital increase of the company itself, i.e. of this issuer. The increase in the number of shares is thus explicitly excluded. If securities are now sold short, it is subject to the issued securities, taken as a whole, do not exist.

Let me explain it this way: By means of a securities loan, a security is transferred from the securities lender to the short seller for delivery purposes by means of a securities account transfer, whereby the short seller is only obliged to return securities of the same type. According to the securities lending agreement, eco-

nomic and civil law ownership[5] arises for the securities borrower with the transfer, which is disposed of by the subsequent delivery process; nevertheless, the securities lender has not yet relinquished his ownership of the lent security on the basis of the securities lending agreement, just as he continues to receive all "fruits" from it and continues to bear the associated price risk for the share. The conversion of the security into a loan in kind therefore reconverts ownership of the security into claims with the result of configurable quantities of securities in circulation, which any delivery cover is again able to provide up to its total quantity itself. These rights of disposal must be questioned, because only the vehicle of securities lending enables the short seller, who is obliged to deliver, to initiate a delivery process at all, because otherwise a simple delivery default would occur.

Third-party lenders therefore regularly come on the scene and are constantly on the market to slightly increase their return through securities lending. And it is to be suspected that securities lenders acting as third-party lenders cause more harm than good to their end clients at investment funds, pension funds, etc. with the securities lending they make possible, at least in price-sensitive securities, these groups of people have to accept price losses resulting from short-selling activities, which the low additional earnings often cannot make up for.

A review of several sales prospectuses of investment fund companies has shown that securities lending transactions are regularly mentioned here and are therefore not an isolated case,

---

5 see also 2.1, 3.6, 10.1

since the paragraphs always refer to the fact that the assets held in the investment fund can be transferred to third parties on a loan basis for a fixed or indefinite period of time in return for a market-based fee. Therefore, the investment-fund sales prospectuses must be viewed critically from this perspective.

2.1 The paradox

The de facto absence of securities in circulation after short selling in the banking system, these papers must paradoxically be recovered out of this banking system itself to deliver the short sales.

It manifests; the short sale deliveries made through securities lending only lead to exchanged stocks between the supplying banks at the securities clearing bank, but a negative total balance pot is created in the banking system, which is made up of all short sales delivered and not returned. This result shows that the securities borrower and short seller, as the beneficiary under economic and also civil law, was able to make a disposition of property in his capacity as non-owner, but also the shortfall of now non-existent securities in the banking system.

Nevertheless, the securities lender remains the owner under the loan agreement, to whom the securities of the same type must be returned. Securities supplied from short sales, as shown, are now no longer available against the actual volume of securities in circulation[6] . This is the issue volume itself, plus all additional short sales made, but these may under no circumstances be serviced out of the issue, as this is inadmissible according to the interpretation of the Stock Exchange Act §32 in connection with the BörsZulV §5 paragraph 1. Since the additional quantity generated by short selling does not exist, it must be procured again by repurchase in the market.

The existing regulatory provision ensures, via the construct of securities lending as a perpetual motion machine, that the securities market remains intact as capable of delivery, which, however, neither the Stock Exchange Act nor the Stock Exchange Admission Ordinance allow to be done in accordance with the law.

Note: The standard master agreement on securities lending states under item 3 on the transfer of securities that with the delivery the unrestricted ownership passes to the borrower, borne out by the German Fiscal Code (§ 39 paragraph 1 AO[7] , basic case), which assumes that in the case of a securities loan the economic and civil law ownership is attributable to a borrower, the civil law ownership changes with the delivery.

2.2 Poker game

Especially in highly volatile markets, it sometimes resembles a poker game, because the securities that are no longer available now have to be retrieved and covered. No one wants to make

---

6 see also 2.0, 3.6, 10.1

7 Tax code

losses in the process, of course, but to win primarily. Neverthe-
less, many (small investors in the case of funds, pensioners/self
employed persons in the case of pension funds) normally lose in
a game.

If securities, i.e. securities sold short, can no longer be re-
covered at the "previously intended prices", further distortions in
the market could be the result. Erratic price caprices are then
short squeezes that occur repeatedly, which we experienced, for
example, in 2008 in the Volkswagen share with prices of over €
1,000.00 at the peak, which at that time perhaps corresponded to
the equivalent value of the valuation of all important car manu-
facturers worldwide.

2.3 Liquidity Reduction without short sale?

Empirical studies in the past have repeatedly tried to prove
that unauthorised short selling would always be negative overall,
on the one hand for the liquidity of a security and on the other
hand for market efficiency itself.

However, why do proponents of this short-selling investment
strategy argue that only this market behaviour would often be the
first to detect overvalued stocks instead of the market itself? Eco-
nomic research and reports exist nonetheless; as a business
model, short selling is not suitable outside of market making as a
purely interest-driven profit vehicle, also because, technically
speaking, no additional liquidity can be made available and neg-
ative information flows into the price formation anyway.

On the surface, the proactive argumentation of the EU Short Selling Regulation on short selling is certainly given. It is true that high liquidity tends to reduce margins between buying and selling, the spread of a security. In addition, increased market volume should always have a price-dampening effect in both directions in a normal environment, but how if there is no excess liquidity.

It is absolutely recognised that under the regime of market making, market liquidity is guaranteed at all times even under the most extreme market conditions. However, this extremely necessary regulatory provision under the WpHG may only be implemented as an exceptional authorisation in market making, and may by no means be generally applicable.

However, as short selling is common market practice, higher volatilities and price fluctuations are the order of the day, and we are tending to experience increased effects, especially in down markets, assume increasingly frequent erratic price fluctuations.

Short selling must be questioned in principle, whether the additional corrective of price fixing through short selling is waived or the unconditional tradability must be given, it is as superfluous from the investor's point of view as it is susceptible to abuse. In addition, since abuse is highly subtle, its monitoring is not only costly, but also requires strict follow-up of any violations detected.

3. Covered / uncovered short sale

In the past, politicians have always pointed out that everything is under control, that uncovered short selling is forbidden, as heard a long time ago on 17 March 2013 on ZDF, Maybrit Illner - wie gerecht ist Deutschland (How fair is Germany), presented by the then Secretary General of the FDP, Döring.

The previously practised uncovered short sale has been banned in the meantime, but the covered short sale is ultimately also uncovered, since it was sold without existing securities cover. Only the settlement procedure to be followed ensures that technical sales availability is generated in stock exchange trading based on securities lending and that short selling is only allowed based on this - the covered short sale was born. It must always be borne in mind that securities lending is not accompanied by a definitive transfer of ownership, but only by a temporary transfer of possession in order to enable the technical delivery of securities. Covered or the now prohibited uncovered short sale: "the short seller would in any case not yet have acquired ownership of the short-sold security at the time of sale[8] ". Leaving aside the risk aspects for the short seller, it must be stated that the covered short sale only needs the fig leaf of a secured delivery of securities in order not to be objected to. A short seller, regardless of whether it is an institutional or private client or even the bank itself as a proprietary trader, does not have any delivery worries, the banks

8 Thomas Laurer: The Short Sale of Shares. Delimitation, Forms and Regulatory Implications. In: Zeitschrift für das gesamte Kreditwesen. 61, No. 19, 2008, p. 984.

take care of "everything in writing" - covering the risk aspects towards the client - and ensure the technically flawless processing, booking and reporting of the business transactions to BaFin. A certain degree of transparency should therefore be available, but how reliable can BaFin really trust these figures for the market overview?

3.1 BaFin exemption short selling

Here, the WpHG § 30 ff. provides for an exemption regulation by the defined by BaFin. According to this, market makers, liquidity providers and other persons have been exempted from this short selling rule, albeit subject to reporting requirements.

This officially approved short selling is purpose-oriented and provides the securities market with constant liquidity, as laid down in the stock exchange regulations. For example, a market maker or a liquidity provider can and will procure unavailable securities as a short seller by quoting prices.

In this regard, Section 5 of the EU Short Selling Regulation states, inter alia; "While short selling could have negative effects in certain circumstances, under normal market conditions short selling plays an important role in the orderly functioning of financial markets, in particular in relation to market liquidity and efficient price formation."

However, the critical view of short selling can be seen in the later paragraph § 30 of the EU Short Selling Regulation: "If a financial instrument experiences a significant price decline on a

28

trading venue, the competent authority should also be empowered to intervene swiftly, if necessary, to stop short selling of that instrument on the relevant trading venue within its temporarily restrict or request ESMA[9] to impose such restrictions in other jurisdictions in other jurisdictions in order to achieve for a short period of time to prevent an unregulated falling in price for this instrument in question ".

If market technology is able to do this, and in the most favourable of cases this would be a temporarily short-selling bank institution. Therefore, only market maker activities should be allowed for short selling, as a structural technical necessity[10] .

If the regular actual coverage of the quantity of securities in circulation were to be maintained within the banking system, the conditions for the admission of securities, the Stock Exchange Act and the stock exchange regulations would have to be based on this. The German Stock Corporation Act (Aktiengesetz) also contains precise regulations on this in sections 179 - 240, as well as in the reverse case, that of the capital reduction. Everything is therefore well regulated in the normal case.

3.2 Pandora's Box

The provisions of WpHG § 30 ff. are the linchpin of misunderstood market friendliness by the financial supervisory authorities insofar as it opens the door to short selling in the first place.

---

9 European Securities and Markets Authority ESMA

10 see also 2.0, 2.1, 3.6, 10.1

Both the aforementioned market making and the EU Short Selling Regulation should be seen from this perspective, as both assume a business model that can only function on this basis.

The EU Short Selling Regulation's provision for the Stating that "short selling plays an important role in the orderly functioning of financial markets" is acceptable in itself to keep the market liquid, but it is the door opener to short selling per se.

As has already been shown, outside of market making, a short seller only needs to have a securities lending portfolio beforehand in order to be able to sell short. But once this securities lending inventory is available through his bank or broker, securities can flow out through sale, and all short sales then in turn taken together, up to the total amount of all securities lending agreements in the market for a security that can be covered within the customer's credit lines. Moreover, these can indeed be such huge amounts of securities that, comparatively, the short-selling activities of market makers and liquidity providers are negligible.

A market maker as already described, will provide binding prices for a purchase at all times, assuming that the Short sales that are triggered, entail the delivery obligations described above. The market maker must therefore, within the scope of his activity, continuously strive to balance out short selling positions resulting from price positioning in a controlled manner and as quickly as possible; specified risk parameters regulate this internally at the bank, as well as the compliance departments are responsible for monitoring, and the financial supervisory authority Bafin also requires reporting based on this.

The real problem of short selling, however, is the large num-ber of short sellers who ultimately initiate and act on the customer side below the reporting threshold and outside the market maker area described. Seen as a whole, considerable short selling stocks can build up through short selling activities, often com-pletely unnoticed and bypassing BaFin supervision, which, as de-scribed, are ultimately withdrawn from the primary securities cy-cle and can cause considerable market turbulence. So despite an existing reporting requirement, as the thresholds of the reporting requirement per client are defined from 0.2% of the net short po-sition, and this is, in short, the offsetting of all short positions against long positions, including all derivative positions in finan-cial instruments whose performance depends on the performance of the respective share, divided by the total number of shares is-sued.

3.3 Stop Loss Order

The use of a stop-loss order is often mentioned in the media as a way for investors to protect themselves from unexpected neg-ative price movements in volatile markets. It is certainly not wrong to protect invested capital, but investors often pay a high price for doing so, especially since stop-loss orders that are placed too tightly could always be filled in volatile markets and only a short time later possibly be back where they were stopped out.

If the investor basically does not want this, provided he is fundamentally convinced of his investment, he must run increased risks in order not to be constantly forced out of the market, i.e. be robust enough to then bear and endure risks to a certain degree. Here, too, one can see that without the presence of securities that are normally not on the market, short selling creates artificial market volume, which in turn either compels the investor to actionism or simply has a damaging effect.

3.4 Set pseudo limits

The recommendations repeatedly circulated in Internet forums not to allow anyone else to dispose of one's own securities holdings and to back up sell orders with pseudo-limits make one prick up one's ears. Primarily, this expresses a distrust of custodian banks and credit institutions, but this is unfounded. By setting a sell limit, it is indeed possible for the client to protect a security from unauthorised, even accidental, access by his custodian bank. This position would thus be blocked for a stock market sale, even if only up to an executable phantom price, and only sellable at this price, i.e. protected from an order execution by market remoteness. This pseudo-securities order could be set up inexpensively nowadays, since banks and brokers often charge no or only low order fees for it, and is accessible online at any time in most cases.

3.5 Alternative regulation registered shares

In contrast to the customer-initiated pseudo-limit on existing bearer shares, which are transferred from the seller to the buyer by agreement and transfer, registered shares would also only be protected from short sale delivery access on the part of the customer insofar as they can, if desired, be registered in the company's share register in favour of the shareholder. This is carried out electronically today. On second thought, it is also the case with registered shares that a short sale in this share continues to take place in the market or through the market, only that delivery access to protected customer holdings is excluded.

3.6 Securities in circulation

It should be noted here that the securities in circulation is "The central criterion of all". Everything must be measured against this. The securities clearing and deposit bank, as the central custodian, holds the total amount of the securities issue, while the banking system holds the reciprocal amount. Further, after transfer of the securities lending from the lender to the short seller, the lender continues to have the owner status based on the lending agreement, but now the borrower as short seller is de facto the economic and civil law owner. This scenario is technically conditioned and unavoidable, but can only be properly

represented without the existence of short sales. Therefore, deliv-
eries of short sales ultimately reduce the available tradable secu-
rities in circulation in the banking system. Particularly during the
year between dividend and interest dates, the congruent securities
portfolio coverage in the banking system is continuously not
given. Nevertheless, what does the law say about this?

In the Stock Exchange Act, Section 32 Admission Require-
ment states, "(1) Securities to be traded on the regulated market
of a stock exchange shall require admission or inclusion by the
management, unless otherwise provided in Section 37 or in other
laws."

Section 38 Introduction further states, "(1) the Management
Board shall, upon application by the issuer, decide on the admis-
sion of admitted securities to listing on the regulated market (in-
troduction), at the request of the issuer and inform about the char-
acteristics of the securities to be introduced. The details are reg-
ulated by stock exchange regulations".

Further under § 40 Duties of the issuer: "(1) the issuer of
admitted shares is obliged to apply for admission to the regulated
market for subsequently issued shares of the same class".

From the three preceding paragraphs, it is mandatory to de-
duce that only the number of shares applied for by the issuer and
approved by the stock exchange management, as in the reverse
case of a capital reduction, can be included in stock exchange
trading and limits the quantity of shares that can be made avail-
able for securities trading. This also applies for non-tradable free
float resulting from fixed shareholdings, etc. The participation of

34

the issuer is always required in the issue of shares or their increase, as well as a capital reduction in the opposite case.

Nor can the quantity of securities in circulation be included in stock exchange trading through short selling for the excess quantity derived from it to the issue itself[11] .

Market practice ensures the deliverability of the short sale by securities lending. It is deliberately overlooked that the tradability of the securitised issue volume as a whole is no longer given, since short sales are withdrawn from the securities in circulation as a loan in kind and every further short sale would further reduce the remaining securitised securities in circulation, theoretically to zero. Therefore, tradability is only possible for the part of the securities in circulation not disposed of by short sale, which, however, is not and cannot be taken into account from a technical trading point of view as securitised deposited (still tradable) or deposited (disposed of as short sale - no longer tradable), furthermore, securities delivery is technically impossible anyway. This established problem cannot be eliminated due to the existence of short sales; the securitised securities are therefore only tradable against the remaining issue quantity, issued by the issuers. Overall, it is always only the quantity of securities in circulation itself that is tradable and thus deliverable at all. Against this background, the actual dubiousness of short selling becomes apparent, since more market volume can never be created than is available through the securities issue. This incontro-

---

11 see also 2.0, 2.1, 10.1

vertible observation leaves no room for advocating and permitting short selling at all.

3.7 Corporate crisis and short sale

A company in crisis must first do everything possible to ensure that the economic situation improves. This can be a broad package of measures, starting with cost reduction, improvement/renewal of products, sales offensives as well as other things to get out of a predicament. In any case, the company will continue to exist, in the crisis, despite the crisis, etc., until the turnaround is achieved. With the return of success, the situation would have improved, and depressed stock market quotations would naturally rise again. A short seller sees it differently, who only sees a crisis, a crisis-like situation at a company or would also find other reasons, for example, could take an announced but questionable capital measure of a company as an occasion and decide to sell short. Although the short seller may not necessarily have the goods to sell, this would not be an obstacle in the current stock market environment.

3.8 Short sale statistics

A wide range of information is available on the Internet if the short sale reporting thresholds have been exceeded. In Germany, this can be traced free of charge in the Bundesanzeiger (Federal Gazette), via www.bundesanzeiger.de

Further fee-based comprehensive securities short-selling statistics/information are available to the market, for example, via www.marketplace.spglobal.com/en/datasets/securities-finance-(18), an international financial information company. These can be accessed by institutional investors for their professional work on a daily basis, for many thousands of internationally traded shares.

4. Securities lending

Through securities lending, the "stock reallocation out of the total pot of circulating stock pieces" described in the chapter "Paradox of Short Selling" takes place, as was shown in the example of the XYZ Company. Stocks can therefore only be made available to the borrower for delivery in terms of accounting. It has also already been mentioned that a covered short sale may only be made if there is an existing securities lending agreement.

Therefore, short sellers must enter into contractual assurances with securities lenders in advance that allow them to access certain securities for delivery purposes.

As a rule, institutional investors make parts of their portfolios available for securities lending in order to achieve a small additional margin. This is done by transferring portfolios from the lender's bank to a securities lending pool that can be used by the lender.

In the meantime, securities clearing banks, Clearstream Banking AG for example since 2009, have also made their own securities lending systems available to the affiliated banks for securities lending brokerage.

4.1 The securities lending itself

While the previous articles on the short sale served to describe it, I would now like to deal with the all-important securities lending, through which a short sale can be triggered for settlement, i.e. for the delivery of securities. In principle, it should perhaps be noted that securities lending is not expressly regulated as a loan in §598 of the German Civil Code (BGB)[12] (securities lending as an internationally used term), rather it is a loan in kind according to § 607 of the German Civil Code, since only nonidentical securities can be returned and the return transfer of the same type and quantity to the lender takes place or is possible.

As a rule, securities are nowadays always held in collective custody, i.e. they are deposited with securities clearing com-

---

12 Civil Code

panies.

In Germany, this is Clearstream Banking AG, a company of Deutsche Börse AG. The bank's securities account is transferred to the buyer based on an electronic delivery booking instruction from the seller.

The servicing of a short sale, since it can no longer be withdrawn from the short seller's own securities account due to the lack of available cover, it can only be serviced from a securities lending account of the seller's custodian bank, as already explained, without any delay in delivery, i.e. at the agreed delivery date, the value date. Later, the securities lending transaction must be reversed in accordance with the contract on the agreed return date, whereby the terms can range from daily callable to fixed term.

A short seller will return his securities loan on time or as early as possible for cost reasons. As a rule, this can be done after a short position has been covered in the cash market, simultaneously with the resulting delivery as of two-day value date. The securities lending fees will be charged to the short seller after completion of the transaction.

5   CFDs as derivatives

CFDs are a financial product that came into being because of the stamp duty introduced in England in 1986. Until then, securities trading had been the basis for the levying of stamp duty, but since then the construct of a CFD ("contract for difference") has enabled the tax-free offsetting of price differences between a buyer and a seller via their broker. It is not surprising that CFDs are very popular today and are traded worldwide, although they are no longer tax-exempt.

5.1 CFD trading via CFD brokers

In the case of a bank custody account disposal, executed as a stock exchange sale or as a custody account transfer, banks and credit institutions always check for custody account coverage. This ensures compliance with the total amount of securities in circulation.

The market technique of the CFD broker is different, although, of course, strict business conduct must be observed on the part of the client, with the exclusive focus on monetary liquidity through margin deposits, as this is the decisive medium in the broker/customer relationship. Open contracts are subject to strict margin management by the broker, since positions can only be entered into at all by depositing margin, which may differ from broker to broker with regard to the leverage used on the capital invested and for the product traded. Profits and losses incurred (the settlement of differences) are calculated immediately, i.e. with every price change and against the cash clearing account, and the closing level is determined from open contracts. Every second, the client sees the following monetary values for open positions:

- *Cash account balance*
- *Margin balance*
- *Profit/Loss from open positions*
- *Overall balance*
- *Close-out level of all open positions*

As long as sufficient cash is available or can be replenished in a timely manner, i.e. by bank transfer usually with a lead time of a few hours up to one day, by instant transfer or by credit card instruction immediately, the CFD broker usually allows the opening or existence of CFD positions, regardless of whether it is a long or short position. Since 2017, private investors are no longer obliged to make additional margin payments over and above the capital invested; insufficient margin cover inevitably leads to a position being closed out.

5.2 CFD short selling

As shown above, the CFD broker may have client short positions derived from price quotation, which for reasons of position covering is immediately put through into the market.

The CFD broker acts as a broker or market maker and participates through commissions paid and the margins earned on the countertrade.

Unlike the classic securities commission business of banks and credit institutions, the CFD business is not a pure brokerage business towards the customer, but is often distinct as market making, through own price setting and position management at the broker itself.

In doing so, the CFD broker takes over the corresponding counter-position of the client in his books. At the same time and congruently, the closing out in the market takes place for the purpose of own risk neutrality, which maps the short sale.

As shown, it is these clear interdependencies with the original share in the cash market that make this "underlying" as a share CFD at the broker exactly the same as the original share in terms of price performance, economic characteristics such as dividends and subscription rights, without, however, having direct shareholder rights.

These matching characteristics of a CFD to a share in the cash market make it clear that the quantity of securities in circulation, previously described as fixed, is also indirectly affected by CFD activities, which is "attacked" in the case of a short sale if sales take place without positive CFD inventory cover. Therefore, it remains to be noted that only under the constellation of positive inventories, also at the CFD broker, a sale order leaves the quantity of securities in circulation untouched.

5.3 Transparency obligation

In addition to the prohibition of uncovered short selling, which also applies here, the private CFD trader is also subject to transparency obligations and must publish the net short position in the Federal Gazette for equity CFDs as well as for equities in general if the relevant reporting thresholds are exceeded or not reached, although this can only be done electronically[13] . However, since these are reporting thresholds of 0.2% or more of the number of shares issued, previously referred to as net short positions, at least private investors will not be affected by this due to the magnitudes involved.

6.   Algorithm trading

While in the previous chapters we dealt with the short seller as a non-owner, we now come to a comparable scenario, because many banking institutions have been engaged in the business of algorithm trading for several years.

In this programme trading, buy and sell orders are issued automatically on the basis of fixed parameters, flash quickly and without any human intervention into the electronic stock exchange's trading book, changed or removed from it. If computer programmes identify opportunities to sell short, this will happen without the operating institution actually having the corresponding securities holdings.[14] In this automated settlement the loan process can, but does not necessarily have to be intervened in.

13 BaFin - Letter, updated 1.3.2012: Frequently asked questions on the notification and publication obligations for holders of net short positions

14 possible on the basis of the EU Short Selling Regulation of 2012 if organisational arrangements (securities lending) have been made in advance.

The bookings are made automatically, the borrowing requirement is quantified and communicated to the custodian bank, and any reporting is triggered systematically. A mandatory prerequisite for these trading activities is the audit of the trading book by Compliance in accordance with the EU Short Selling Regulation.

7. Index trading

The Dax40 spot index[15], which is determined by the stock exchange every second, is the decisive prerequisite for much else. The prices are supplied in electronic XETRA stock exchange trading from the 40 Dax stocks themselves, then pre- and post-trade every minute from the listed prices that track the "LDax"[16] (Late Dax).

As a data feed of the stock exchange, the available Dax40 index now finds its way into proprietary trading systems at banks and brokerage houses worldwide, in which the real price image of the index can now be reproduced for investors at any time through derived bid and ask prices, thus making this index tradable to the greatest possible extent and also worldwide.

---

15 ISIN DE0008469008

16 ISIN: DE0001717049

For index volumes traded here, investors on the Eurex derivatives exchange can build up cover positions in the DAX future[17], on all sides. Risk coverage is possible for the market participants here, and this is also the actual interaction between the DAX spot index and the DAX futures whose quarterly maturities are set in March, June, September and December in accordance with the international standard, in each case due on the 3rd Friday as the major expiry date, on which the forward premium existing over the term is reduced again by "hypothetical[18] financing costs at money market interest rate level" until the expiry date of the futures and whose contract is closed out and expires on the expiry date at the established DAX spot index itself.

The interdependencies of the cash market and the index futures are reflected in the exchange price determinations on the one hand and the price developments from the index futures contract on the other. Price developments can thus emanate from the cash market as well as from the futures market itself and can be price determining. Since "the price of the DAX future is also determined by supply and demand, deviations of the DAX future from the DAX40 index can occur in exceptional situations and volatile market phases[19]."

---

17 ISIN DE0008469594

18 Flatex - https://www.flatex.de/service/faqs/#faqQ_411

19 still at 18

8.   Derivatives trading

Since the start of futures trading in 1990 with the then German Futures Exchange (now Eurex), a securities derivatives market has become increasingly established in Germany, some of which have unique selling points worldwide. In the meantime, some Hundreds of thousands of derivatives tradable as securities have been developed for the investment market. These are available across all product groups in a wide range of product types that are in high demand. These listed financial instruments are forward transactions that refer to certain underlyings and whose market price is often disproportionately derived from them, and which are therefore suitable both for hedging against price losses and for speculating on price gains of the underlying. These are mainly certificates on securities, share baskets, indices and other financial instruments, as well as options on underlying assets to buy or sell them. The stock and derivatives markets are therefore closely intertwined and inseparable, as they are mutually dependent. This cycle cannot be broken.

The respective characteristics of the product properties of a derivative therefore already have a considerable direct or indirect influence on the volume of securities in circulation, since the risks from securities issued by derivative issuing houses must be kept risk-neutral by them.

9. Price development

After short-selling attacks, a security often finds itself at a much lower level in terms of price and the price/book ratio (P/B ratio) is significantly depressed, even if it is at least in line with market opinion.

In addition to the correctness of the investment decision itself, wise risk management is therefore of great importance and one of the adjusting screws. In the case of short selling with the pocketing of the very same price gains.

That is extremely painful for the investor of a security, if the lower price level resulting from abrupt short selling is to be accepted. The price gains achieved by short sellers would be collected and the shareholding held would initially only be realisable at these market prices at the written-down values in the investor's securities account.

10. The crux of short selling

Short selling is ultimately explosive. It is not only the players on the financial market who can get into trouble, but also companies, financial institutions and states. The best protection against short selling is still good management itself, i.e. healthy finances. Profitable, well-managed and broadly positioned companies should therefore be the least-affected, but even that does not mean an all clear for them. Conversely, poorly managed, unprofitable or even unprofessional communicating companies virtually call for short sellers. In the case of countries, this can be sloppy public finances, or constant spending programmes or even deficit increases are breeding grounds for short selling.

Changed ratings are always the straw that breaks the camel's back, as the permanent crisis in the stumbling countries of the Eurozone teaches us. What all these constellations have in common is that short selling of securities can therefore act as an accelerant in critical times.

10.1 Securities must be freely tradable (BörsZulV §5.1)

Negative developments on the capital markets can have many causes and reasons. These can be undesirable developments in companies, worsened profit prospects, losses, lost lawsuits, deteriorating ratings for bond issuers, etc. The crucial thing is that investors always keep an accurate picture of the situation, as they always keep up to date with their investments. For a shareholder, for example, this can mean that he or she closely examines the company, the figures, the annual reports and the business outlook, according to the textbooks as a rule always before an investment is made or continuously afterwards, perhaps attending general meetings, etc.

On the stock exchange, it is not just two fundamentally conflicting market participants who are coming together - that has always been the case. Now, with the aforementioned short seller, diametrically different interests are added to the mix.

While an investor always has the pros and cons of "his investment" before his eyes, he knows his risk, his personal risk parameters that he is willing to bear, and his expectations. If the need for action becomes apparent, the investor can also position himself with a decision to sell, which may only be reserved for him as the owner; he bears the economic risk from the investment.

The short seller, on the other hand, sees everything from the point of view of a short-term actor, or analysts' opinion that a sale is necessary based on analyses. At the external asset and without ultimately own property rights, non-owners now decide on the weal and woe of others and their financial investments, and there is unauthorised market intervention through short selling.

This handling is seen critically, since short sales after their delivery ultimately reduce the quantity of securities in circulation/issuance in a questionable manner. Can it be legally okay that a securitised security is withdrawn from securities trading in the case of simultaneous short selling and the associated securities lending with the effect of reducing the issue[20] , and can an agreement between securities lending partners be regulated in a legally sound manner at all against this background? This is clearly negated by the Exchange Admission Regulation (Börs-ZulV) § Five Para.1, which states on the tradability of securities: The securities must be freely tradable.

---

20 see also 2.0, 2.1, 3.6

However, this requirement can only be fulfilled in the case of a portfolio sale and is only conditionally possible for the short sale through a prior lending agreement and transfer of securities to the short seller. As already explained in paragraph 3.6, the free tradability of this subset of the securities issue disposed of by short selling is then at the same time no longer given, since this securities holding has resulted in a loan in kind in accordance with §607 of the German Civil Code (BGB).

Therefore, tradability made possible without a short sale ban leads to non-deliverability, as stated. Interestingly, this scenario is exactly congruent with today's situation. There is no short sale ban today. Moreover, it is precisely this view that makes a short-selling ban argumentatively justified and necessary.

10.2 Self-service effect

It should be noted that ultimately, intentionally or unintentionally, there is a concomitant self-service effect caused by the global traders' backdrop, especially through their systemic stock market integration and networking, which is taking place on the backs of others. These are first the shareholders, who not only have to bear the economic risk from the market price changes that occur anyway. Artificially added illegal share volumes from short selling and the effects of index trading have to be endured by the shareholder without complaint.

10.3 Shareholder culture

Politicians keep saying that economic prosperity can ulti-mately only be achieved through participation in companies in the economy itself. As correct as this statement is in principle, there are unfortunately many obstacles to this, such as market conditions. High volatilities, spectacular company bankruptcies, constant additional threats of taxation and much more have to be accepted; also, burst stock market bubbles after the Internet boom in 2000 or the Lehman shock in the financial crisis from 2008 onwards are still fresh in our memories today.

Shareholders who took part in the privatisation of Deutsche Telekom from 1998 onwards will hardly be able to get excited about shares any more, as they will not be able to recoup the sub-scription prices they once paid.

It is not only that the flat rate withholding tax of 25%, which has been in force since 2009, affects investors, but also that the additional solidarity tax of 5.5% will continue to apply to top earners from 2020. It is also the "silo taxation of investment in-come" as a non-existent possibility of not offsetting gains and losses from the various types of income from securities. In addi-tion, in 2022, the further restricting tax loss deduction was added in a tightening and groundless manner. The discussions about the tax level itself and the financial transaction tax as a non-profit-based turnover tax on financial transactions need to be mentioned further.

The unequal treatment of share investments compared to the productive capital of private companies in the case of inheritance should not go unmentioned, because the focus in the case of shares is on full taxation according to allowances, while in the case of the latter, assets are gently transferred to the next generation under the premise of preserving jobs.

Overall, this is not an environment that could not be improved from an investor's point of view. Nevertheless, one should not ask oneself why the number of shareholders in Germany has been declining for years and why nothing can stop it. And so the DAI, Deutsches Aktieninstitut, Frankfurt am Main, noted several years ago that the number of direct equity investors had fallen by 26.7% from the record level in 2000 to Q1/2013 [21]had declined. Confidence in the share is only slowly returning in 2015[22] , although this is largely due to the low interest rate environment that will persist until 2022/2023.

11. Imbalance of the financial markets

The real economy and the financial economy have been diverging for a number of years and must therefore move towards each other again in order to reduce distortions, as has been demonstrated not least since the financial crisis of 2008 with the Lehmann bankruptcy has clearly shown when the world financial system stood on the brink of the abyss. However, further bubbles

---

21   Brief study by Deutsches Aktieninstitut Q1/2013

22   DAI study for 2015

have again been created by the continuously lowered interest rate level[23] worldwide until 2022 and the further increase in debt overall. It is already dramatic and so no one really knows when this new bubble will unload, but not whether it will happen. The collapse of two American regional banks and the economic collapse of Credit Suisse in March 2023 are already showing this as distortions in bank balance sheets, due to unnoticed maturity transformations in the interest rate environment.

According to the BIS VII. OTC derivatives statistics, taken from the Deutsche Bundesbank's banking statistics of 15 December 2022, the global market of the 74 market-leading banks of the G10 countries by notional amounts was €384.767 billion in 2008, but already €607.691 billion in 2022.

According to the ECB, the M3 money supply in the euro area grew from 9.401 trillion euros to 16.090 trillion euros in the same period. Price increases and growing inflation rates must be noted.

Rapidly rising figures can also be seen in the national debt, which has continued to pile up in the meantime, including the USA with 31.653 trillion (according to the US National Debt Clock of 1.4.2023) and Germany with 2.462 trillion (according to the debt clock of 1.4.2023). Until the start of the Corona pandemic at the beginning of 2020, Germany will manage to structurally maintain and slightly reduce its debt, but since the start of the Ukraine war, the debt clock has been ticking faster.

In the case of the USA, all dams have obviously broken with

---

23 e.g. reduction of the ECB reference interest rate to 0 % on 11.3.2016

a high increase in government debt of trillions of US dollars per year. The credit expansions that have been shown are causing the money supply to continue to grow steadily. These are not good omens for being able to keep excessive financial markets under control at all, which would make future restructuring possible and prevent capital misallocations, as was certainly the case in Germany in the real estate sector until recently.

The central banks' policies have provided the wrong guidance, but it is too late to question that now.

12. Rethinking required

First, it must be stated that an "over-revved financial merry-go-round" will not easily find its way back to normal speed. The decisive factor will be whether changes are wanted, not least politically, how they are subsequently implemented and tackled, and to what extent the actors are willing to cooperate. Ultimately, debts must be repaid. Cuts are unavoidable. Many things should and must be done differently in the future, a large catalogue of tasks will have to be worked through, often familiar things will have to be done without and cuts will be unavoidable if the environment is to improve.

As far as the financial market is concerned, a streamlining of the banking apparatus is probably inevitable and must be brought back into line with the general economy, whereby the banks must once again internalise their mission as servants of the economy, to ensure the supply of money and payment transactions, to accept funds and manage assets, to be available to the economy with loans and services of all kinds, and to be profitable without taking on excessive risks, as has often happened in the past. Finally yet importantly, banking supervision should be mentioned, which recognises risks more effectively and better in advance.

It is evident that some banking businesses are on the rise. Other things are taken care of anyway through increased financial resources in accordance with the stricter Basel capital guidelines. Nevertheless, why does excessive government spending always cause banks to stumble? The acceptance of risks of any kind must always be clearly weighed up, strict risk management and the observance of matching maturities should exclude interest rate distortions as far as possible; and thus ultimately effectively secure bank balance sheets.

Political rethinking is called for as to how things can continue at all on the "debt front" of the states as a whole, how government spending can be financed in the future. Who can ultimately take investment risks "on the books"? Pension funds, private old-age provision, at least banks, can only do this to a limited extent according to current knowledge, that much is clear. Society as a whole is facing systemic questions that can no longer be displaced. The QE programme[24] initiated by the European Central Bank until 2022/2023 to buy back issued public bonds of European debtor countries with many billions of euros per month

---

24 ECB quantitative easing programme

was ultimately not the solution, but in retrospect presents itself as the problem. The flooding of the markets with liquidity was dev-astating for savers all these years, who paid for the stumbling euro countries with zero interest rates and inflation. Today, in an environment of high inflation rates and the effects of the Ukraine war, parts of the financial industry are once again facing the shambles of failed investment decisions in anticipation of bailouts.

12.1 Roll back regulation

The continuous addition of financial products in recent years has constantly required new adjustments to the regulation of the business environment; EU regulations had to be imple-mented at the national level. With the reduction of business on the one hand, and the rethinking of the range of products on the other, there are hopefully good starting points in the financial industry, so that overall, regulation does not have to be expanded, but is reduced.

For this, increased capitalisation of banking institutions is indispensable. There is a need for action on a general ban on short selling. On the other hand, securities lending for the pur-pose of regular securities delivery settlement of spot and forward transactions in a functioning securities market is extremely nec-essary; other securities lending transactions aimed at this as a vehicle for short selling are unacceptable.

As already stated, it should be noted with regard to the EU Short Selling Regulation: the functioning of the markets and their liquidity supply is valued more highly than shareholder protection. Securities that may be traded on the regulated market are only admitted by the management of the stock exchange, and in addition to this, §5.1 of the Stock Exchange Admission Regulation is based on the condition that securities must be freely tradable.

12.2 Reduce costs

A ban on short selling outside the scope of the market maker would, as mentioned, not only strengthen the shareholder, but also greatly simplify the regulation of securities transactions. An elimination of unnecessary banking applications for short selling and securities lending could follow. In the reporting system for securities transactions and finally in the supervision of securities transactions by BaFin, there would be considerable potential for reducing the workload. Many things would be eliminated, including costs. The banks would be relieved of material, personnel and auditing costs.

13. Cum/Ex trades

Securities transactions that are regularly traded up to the dividend separation date; they are dividend-entitled (cum dividend) and include the securities delivery as well as the dividend payment; transactions traded later are settled ex-dividend.

It was precisely at this interface that problems arose with the existence of short sales, which still occupy the courts today. If available, non-dividend-bearing securities were smuggled into the market through short selling before the dividend date, the tax certificates of the purchasing bank derived from this got out of control. The traceability of dividend entitlements was no longer given for all parties involved, as the certifying bank was not at the same time responsible for the deduction of capital gains tax, which was only addressed again by the legislator in 2009 as a legal loophole that still needed to be remedied and whose final settlement then took place in 2012 by switching the taxation of dividends from the issuer to the custodian bank.

In the past, short sales that were open at the time via the dividend deadline, which are only now being dealt with in court as Cum/Ex transactions, have caused high macroeconomic damages in the alleged billions from unjustifiably declared dividend and tax certificates, precisely because of incorrect handling of this issue in the banking system and by the tax authorities. Finally yet importantly, banking supervisors and legislators may ask themselves, why problems in this environment had not been addressed earlier; indications of this were available for a long time and the history of this can be traced in the minutes of the fourth

Bundestag Investigation Committee of 2017. Until 2011, a cum purchasing bank was always responsible for the correctness of a tax certificate issued by it and was therefore well advised, if a delivery of securities from off-exchange transactions that was open beyond the dividend date was determined, to have the seller additionally present the tax and dividend certificate that he himself had received, otherwise to consider subsequent taxation. Any deviation due to the debit balance of an end customer always had to be checked very carefully so that on balance no additional refundable dividend certificates could be circulated by the bank itself. The amended capital gains tax deduction procedure from 2012, regulated in the UCITS-IV Conversion Act of 2011, now led to central responsibility at the custodian bank for the forwarding of dividends to the end customer, for the tax deduction and for the issuing of tax certificates for submission to the tax authorities on the basis of the custody account bookkeeping located in the banking area and the balances determined from this on the separation date. The portfolio representation of a security by the securities clearing and deposit bank is mainly confronted with all customer balances to which the income is to be forwarded with the deduction of capital gains tax and solidarity surcharge. In addition, there are those from undelivered stock exchange transactions of the stock exchange clearing system which, as a result, are booked into the customer's portfolio up to the cum date (entitlement day or also separation day), entitled to dividends on the buyer side, just as these are no longer taken into account on the respective seller side for this stock exchange transaction, because a dividend is no longer due there. Undelivered off-exchange transactions or open securities lending transactions over a dividend date have since been debited with the gross dividend in order to exclude unjustified tax refunds.

14 The role of BaFin:

The coverage of the short selling business area is an integral part of the securities supervision of BaFin Berlin/Bonn/Frankfurt. Depending on the subject matter, the office focuses on short selling monitoring, for which reporting obligations via the banking system must be fulfilled within the framework of regulation, whereby the EU Short Selling Regulation 236/2012, which has been in force since 2012, forms the basis. Paragraph five of the introduction states:

"In order to overcome the current fragmentation against which some Member States have taken divergent measures and to limit the possibility of competent authorities taking divergent measures, a harmonised approach is needed to address the potential risks of short selling and credit default swaps. The rules to be introduced should address the identified risks without unduly diminishing the benefits that short selling offers to market quality and efficiency. While short selling could have negative effects in certain circumstances, under normal market conditions short selling plays an important role in the orderly functioning of financial markets, particularly in terms of market liquidity and efficient price formation."

For this reason, unfortunately, a complete ban on short selling was waived within the framework of the EU Short Selling Regulation. As already mentioned, the European Directive overrides existing German law, and allows, what was never allowed before and to date in Germany. The reference to the Stock Exchange Act and the Stock Exchange Admission Ordinance should be mentioned again.

BaFin follows the legal mandate by applying the EU Short Selling Regulation, but no longer questions existing German law. Instead of working towards changes in the European legislator and acting there as a securities supervisor as an important source of information, everything is left to rest, although there is a great need for action.

15. Concluding remarks:

As shown, a short selling ban for securities is to be enforced via the vehicle of a securities lending stop for short selling purposes, because additional dynamics and volatility in the markets derived from short selling is homemade. BaFin has now pulled the ripcord twice in 2019 in the case of Wirecard by means of a short-selling ban; on the other hand, nothing at all has happened in the case of Steinhoff, although the price level has fallen by 99.8% in the last few years and short sellers obviously have been able to work their way mercilessly through the share to this day and keep the price under control down to the cent decimal place. The disadvantages of short selling, as well as the fact that it is susceptible to abuse, must be acknowledged, and finally yet importantly, I would like to expressly state once again the noncompliance with laws and regulations. The legal questions raised about short selling are so significant, that they must now be definitively investigated. These problems had been discussed in detail in sections 2.0, 2.1, 3.6, 10.1. Only for this reason, and only in view of a market technique that must be maintained, may only the market making and liquidity provider model according to § 30 WPHG et seq. be tolerated under strict BaFin regulations; it is to be accepted in the overriding overall interest, as it is also appropriate and necessary for this reason. There is no justification for further permitted end-customer short selling of securities, as the available securities in customer securities accounts can be sold at any time. Market making would keep the securities market intact, albeit with reduced liquidity. The volume of securities in circulation, the primary circulation, may not be undermined in the future or otherwise, and the existing volume of securities in circulation would always remain closer to the actual issue volume, taking market making into account.

Systemically, the stock exchanges as part of the financial world have developed rapidly, especially since the establishment of the futures markets. We are moving in an internationally operating exchange world in which the market participants are able to communicate with each other through networking. Moreover, every market participant must fulfil technical market access criteria based on data standards. Stock exchange today means networking, strictly regulated, conditional on requirements and standards, also internationally and continuously interwoven up to the last branches of the settlement and stock exchange systems. Every market participant operates in its own environment, with licensing conditions, requirements, reporting regulations, financial equipment and much, much more. This extends all the way to the bank client himself, even if the interface is made available to him by his bank or broker, predefined as a PC application or as an Internet-based web application; further access options have opened up via mobile data terminals such as laptops and the iPhone®[25] or smartphone.

Market making is explicitly mentioned by the EU Short Selling Regulation, thus confirming Deutsche Börse AG's international trading practices.

Computers and calculators already have a significant influence on the current stock exchange system. Price development and pricing within the system result from the specifications laid down in the rules and regulations and, as a rule, automatically without manual intervention. The interconnectedness of the markets forces everything together and provides for a certain directionality of the market, even if the individual investment decision of each market participant is always given.

This interconnectedness of the markets, the existence of global stock market indices and mandatory market making are the actual price-driving elements of global stock market activity per se. The short-selling scenario is be seen in this larger context, the short-selling ban must be addressed, the factual situation is clear.

---

25 Apple Inc. Mobile digital device

The current legal framework of the stock exchange environment is set, rules that still need be revised, are to be drawn up as quickly as possible and then put into force. Nevertheless, how can this be done, who puts it on the agenda and who is to be held accountable?

Legislator:
Here I see no will for change. Only the left party "Die LINKE" has spoken out against short selling for ideological reasons, as well as for a ban on algorithm trading and for the introduction of a transaction tax.

BaFin:
Here they are fixated on the EU Short Selling Regulation; the existing German law is suspended and at the same time disregarded.

Issuers:
That would be my only hope - issuers should therefore raise the legal issues themselves with the stock exchange operator and the supervisory bodies and have them clarified in their own best interest so that their own shares are subject to a permanent short-selling ban, if necessary by taking legal action. To tackle, clarify and enforce this would be the task of the decade, thus the resistance will be great,

- *It remains exciting and highly interesting!*
- *Moreover, it must be waited for!*